JERALD SIMON

The Dawn
of a New Age

12 Original New Age Piano Solos for Intermediate - late Intermediate Students

JERALD SIMON

Music Motivation®
Cool music that excites, entertains, and educates!

visit http://musicmotivation.com
follow Jerald on Facebook: https://facebook.com/jeraldsimon

Music Motivation® books are designed to provide students with music instruction that will enable them to improve and increase their successes in the field of music. It is also intended to enhance appreciation and understanding of various styles of music from classical to jazz, blues, rock, popular, new age, hymns, and more. The author and publisher disclaim any liability or accountability for the misuse of this material as it was intended by the author.

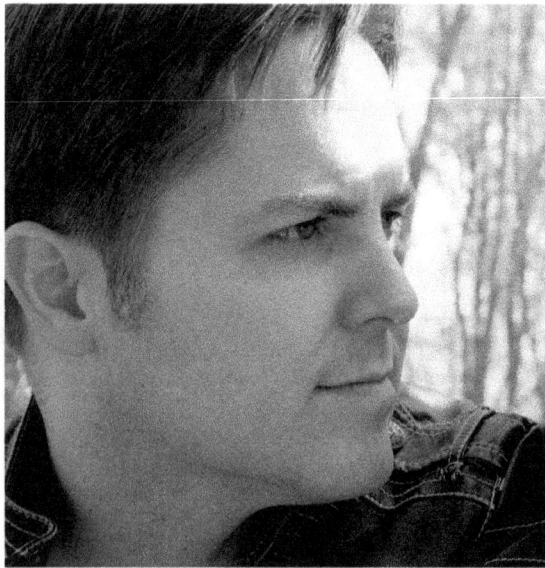

JERALD SIMON

This book is dedicated to my many piano students - young and old alike, who ask for ideas and left hand patterns to create new age sounding music of their own.

Also, to my wife, Suzanne (Zanny), my daughter, Summer, and my son, Preston.

The cover image photography (and family portrait on the back cover) were taken by Wendy Santiano. Visit her website at:

http://www.wendysantiano.com or
https://www.facebook.com/wsantianoauthor

The background photo on the back cover was taken by Jerald Simon

I hope you enjoy "The Dawn of a New Age™". With this book, I want to teach piano concepts and skills (left hand New Age patterns) to better help pianists create music of their own. This book is graded in that each piano solo gradually becomes more difficult (the easiest pieces are at the beginning of the book and the most difficult ones are at the end of the book).

The pieces in this book will help you learn fun, piano skills (such as music theory, technique, transposing, improvising, and composing) through upbeat and cool sounding piano selections composed by me - your personal Music Mentor™ - Jerald Simon.

Have fun with the music!

CONNECT with Jerald

http://musicmotivation.com/jeraldsimon
https://facebook.com/jeraldsimon
http://youtube.com/jeraldsimon
http://linkedin.com/in/jeraldsimon
https://twitter.com/jeraldsimon
http://cdbaby.com/artist/jeraldsimon
http://reverbnation.com/jeraldsimon
jeraldsimon@musicmotivation.com

CONTACT Music Motivation

Music Motivation®
Cool music that excites, entertains, and educates!™
Music Motivation®
P.O. Box 1000
Kaysville, UT 84037-1000
http://musicmotivation.com
https://facebook.com/musicmotivation
https://twitter.com/musicmotivation
info@musicmotivation.com

First Printing 2014 - Printed in the United States of America - 10 9 8 7 6 5 4 3 2 1 - Simon, Jerald - Music Motivation® - The Dawn of a New Age - $18.95 US/ $20.95 Canada - Soft cover spiral bound book - ISBN-13: 978-0-9835568-7-9 ; MM00001016

Music Motivation® is a registered trademark

Welcome to *"The Dawn of a New Age™"* by JERALD SIMON

There are 12 original new age piano solos composed by Jerald Simon in this book. They were composed for the intermediate to late intermediate piano students. As with all of Jerald's original piano music, he teaches music theory through each song. Jerald's books are not method books - simply fun, cool piano solos that Teach Music Theory - The Fun Way™. It is his hope that pianists of all ages will enjoy playing these new age piano solos. The theory in the introduction of this book is presented to help piano students and piano teachers understand the theory of new age left hand patterns and how to use them to create music of their own.

"My purpose and mission in life is to motivate myself and others through my music and writing, to help others find their purpose and mission in life, and to teach values and encourage everyone everywhere to do and be their best." - Jerald Simon

A message from Jerald to piano students and parents:

If you come to piano lessons each week and walk away only having learned about music notation, rhythm, and dots on a page, then I have failed as a Music Mentor™. Life lessons are just as important, if not more important than music lessons. I would rather have you learn more about goal setting and achieving, character, dedication, and personal improvement. To have you learn to love music, appreciate it, and play it, is a wonderful byproduct you will have for the rest of your life - a talent that will enrich your life and the lives of others. To become a better musician is wonderful and important, but to become a better person is more important.

As a Music Mentor™ I want to mentor students to be the very best they can be. If you choose not to practice, you essentially choose not to improve. This is true in any area of life. Everyone has the same amount of time allotted to them. What you choose to do with your time, and where you spend your time, has little to do with the activities being done and more to do with the value attached to each activity.

I believe it's important to be well-rounded and have many diverse interests. I want students to enjoy music, to learn to be creative and understand how to express themselves musically - either by creating music of their own, or interpreting the music of others - by arranging and improvising well known music. In addition, I encourage students to play sports, dance, sing, draw, read, and develop all of their talents. I want them to be more than musicians, I want them to learn to become well-rounded individuals.

Above all, I want everyone to continually improve and do their best. I encourage everyone to set goals, dream big, and be the best they can be in whatever they choose to do. Life is full of wonderful choices. Choose the best out of life and learn as much as you can from everyone everywhere. I prefer being called a Music Mentor™ because I want to mentor others and help them to live their dreams.

Your life is your musical symphony. Make it a masterpiece!

Jerald Simon

Left hand New Age patterns

Left hand pattern: 1-5-1-5-1-5-1-5 (e.g. C-G-C-G-C-G-C-G)

This is an example from **Morning Star** (measure 1) on page 6. This left hand pattern rocks back and forth between the 1 and 5 intervals (e.g. 1 = C, and 5 = G).

Left hand pattern: 1-5-8-5-1-5-8-5 (e.g. A-E-A-E-A-E-A-E)

This is an example from **The Sands of Time** (measure 1) on page 9. This left hand pattern is created by playing the first, fifth, and octave intervals (e.g. 1 = A, 5 = E, and 8 = A up an octave above the 1). You can try playing this pattern on every note on the piano.

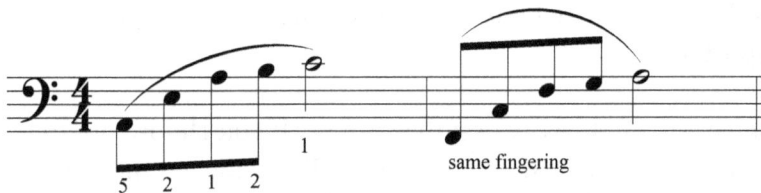

Left hand pattern: 1-5-8-9-10 (e.g. A-E-A-B-C)

This is an example from the piano solo **Reflection** (measure 1) on page 12. This left hand pattern is created by playing the first, fifth, eighth, ninth, and tenth notes from any scale (e.g. 1 = A, 5 = E, 8 = A, 9 = B, and 10 = C).

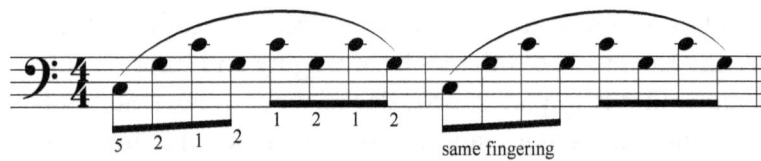

Left hand pattern: 1-5-8-5-8-5-8-5 (e.g. C-G-C-G-C-G-C-G)

This is an example from the piano solo **Song of Serenity** (measure 45) on page 17. This left hand pattern is created by playing the first, fifth and eighth intervals and then rocking back and forth between the fifth and the eighth notes from any scale (e.g. 1 = C, 5 = G, 8 = C).

Left hand pattern: 1-5-8-9-10-9 (e.g. C-G-C-G-C-G-C-G)

This is an example from the piano solo **Downcast** (measure 17) on page 20. This left hand pattern is created by playing the first, fifth, eighth, ninth, and tenth notes from any scale (e.g. 1 = D, 5 = A, 8 = D, 9 = E, 10 = F back to the 9 which is E).

MM00001016

Music that excites, entertains, and educates™

Left hand New Age patterns

Left hand pattern: 1-5-8-1-5-8 (e.g. C-G-C-C-G-C)

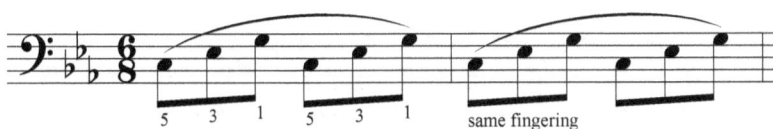

This is an example from the piano solo *Utopia* (measure 45) on page 24. This left hand pattern is created by playing the first, fifth and eighth notes from any scale over and over again in a cycle (e.g. 1 = C, and 5 = G, and 8 = C up an octave above the 1).

Left hand pattern: 1-3-5-1-3-5 (e.g. C-E♭-G-C-E♭-G)

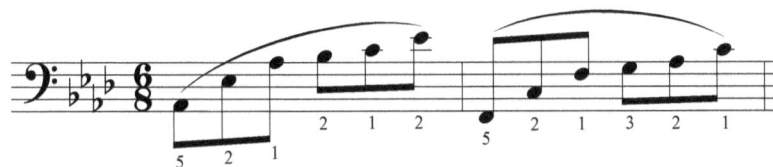

This is an example from the piano solo *The Dawn of a New Age* (measure 1) on page 28. This left hand pattern is easily created by playing the first, third, and fifth, notes from any scale over and over again (e.g. 1 = C, 3 = E♭, and 5 = G.

Left hand pattern: 1-5-8-9-10-12 (e.g. A♭-E♭-A♭-B♭-C-E♭)

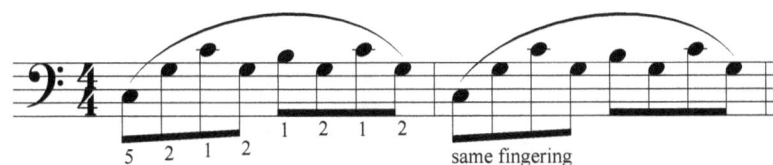

This is an example from the piano solo *Heaven on Earth* (measure 1) on page 32. This left hand pattern is created by playing the first, fifth, eighth, ninth, and tenth notes from any scale (e.g. 1 = A♭, 5 = E♭, 8 = A♭, 9 = B♭, 10 = C, and 12 = E♭).

Left hand pattern: 1-5-8-5-7-5-8-5 (e.g. C-G-C-G-C-G-C-G)

This is an example from the piano solo Tranquility (measure 9) on page 38. This left hand pattern is created by playing the first, fifth, and eighth notes from any scale and then rotating back to the fifth, seventh, fifth, tenth, and fifth notes from any scale (e.g. 1 = C, and 5 = G, and 8 = C up an octave above the 1).

Try playing all of these examples in several keys (preferably in all keys). You should try playing these patterns beginning on every note on the piano (A, B, C, D, E, F, G including all of the sharps and flats). Become familiar with the rhythms and make sure your left hand can keep the pattern going independent of the right hand. When you can do this comfortably in all keys, it will help you tremendously when playing new age music. Have fun with the following 12 new age piano solos. Make music of your own with these simple left hand patterns!

Morning Star

This piano solo uses a *1-5-1-5-1-5-1-5* left hand pattern where the pinkey and thumb rock back and forth creating a steady pulse (e.g. 1 = C and 5 = G repeated over and over).

Gently (M.M. ♩ = c. 110)

by **Jerald Simon**

mf RH crosses over

mp

5 1 5 1 5 1 5 1

pedal ad-lib throughout

f

mf

MM00001016

Morning Star

MM00001016

Copyright © 2014 by Music Motivation® - http://musicmotivation.com

7

Morning Star

MM00001016

The Sands of Time

This piano solo uses a *1-5-8-5-1-5-8-5*; *1-5-8-9-10*, and *1-5-8-5-9-5-10-5* left hand patterns

Gently (♩ = c. 108)   As the sands being blown by the wind

by **Jerald Simon**

pedal ad-lib throughout

The Sands of Time

MM00001016

The Sands of Time

Reflection

This piano solo uses a *1-5-8-9-10* (e.g. A-E-A-B-C - see measure one), and the *1-8-12-15-16-17* (e.g. A-A-E-A-B-C - see measure 25) left hand patterns.

by **Jerald Simon**

MM00001016

Reflection

Reflection

MM00001016

Song of Serenity

This piano solo uses a *1-5-8-5-1-5-8-5* (e.g. A-E-A-E-A-E-A-E - see measure 23); *1-5-8-5-8-5-8-5* (e.g. C-G-C-G-C-G-C-G - see measure 45); and *1-5-8-9-10* (e.g. A-E-A-B-C - see measure 53) left hand patterns.

With Feeling ♩ = 120

by **Jerald Simon**

mf

pedal ad-lib throughout

mf

cresc.

MM00001016

15

Song of Serenity

Song of Serenity

Song of Serenity

MM00001016

Song of Serenity

Downcast

This piano solo uses a *1-5-8-9-10-9* (e.g. D-A-D-E-F-E - see measure 17), and *1-5-8-1-5-8* (e.g. D-A-D-C-G-C - see measure 37) left hand patterns.

by **Jerald Simon**

With Purpose (M.M. ♩ = c. 160)

mf

pedal ad-lib throughout

cresc.

MM00001016

Downcast

Downcast

MM00001016

Utopia

This piano solo uses a *1-5-8-1-5-8* (C-G-C-C-G-C - see measure 45) left hand pattern.

by **Jerald Simon**

Thoughtfully (♩ = c. 120)

mp

pedal ad-lib throughout

MM00001016

Utopia

MM00001016

Utopia

Utopia

Utopia

The Dawn of a New Age

This piano solo uses a *1-3-5-1-3-5* (e.g. C-E♭-G-C-E♭-G - see measure 1) left hand pattern.

by **Jerald Simon**

Flowing (♩ = c. 108-120)

pedal ad-lib throughout

MM00001016

The Dawn of a New Age

The Dawn of a New Age

MM00001016

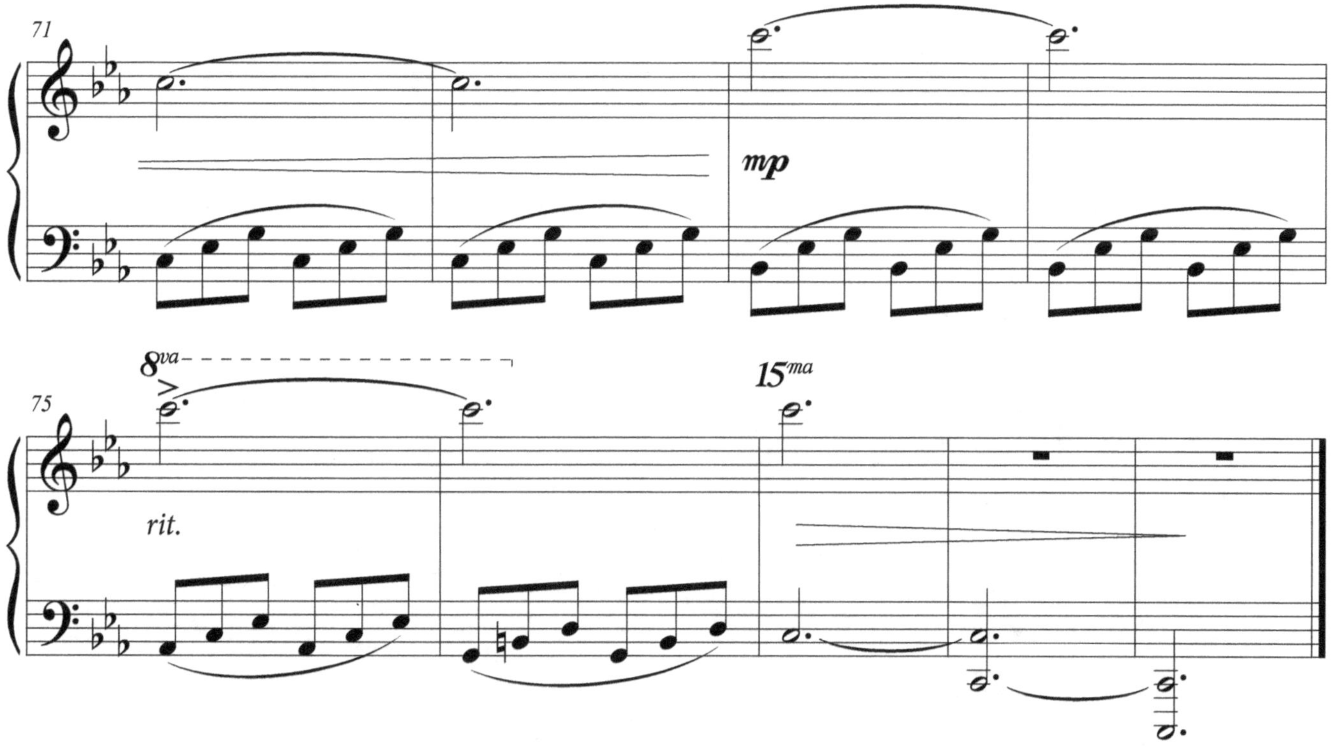
71
mp
75
8va
rit.
15ma

Heaven on Earth

This piano solo uses a *1-5-8-9-10-12* (e.g. A♭,-E♭-A♭-B♭-C-E♭ - see measure 1) left hand pattern.

by **Jerald Simon**

MM00001016

Heaven on Earth

Heaven on Earth

MM00001016

Hereafter

This piano solo uses a *1-3-5-5-3* (e.g. C-E♭-G-G-E♭ - see measure 1) and *1-5-8-5-8-5* (e.g. C-G-C-G-C-G - see measure 9) left hand patterns.

by **Jerald Simon**

pedal ad-lib throughout

MM00001016

Hereafter

MM00001016

Hereafter

Tranquility

This piano solo uses a *1-5-8* (e.g. A-E-A - see measure 1); *1-5-8-9-10* (e.g. A-E-A-B-C - see measure 3); and *1-5-8-5-7-5-8-5* (e.g. C-G-C-G-B-G-C-G - see measure 5) left hand patterns.

by **Jerald Simon**

pedal ad-lib throughout

MM00001016

Tranquility

Tranquility

Destiny

This piano solo uses a *1-8-12-15* (e.g. F-F-C-F-G - see measure 1); *1-5-8-10-12-15* (C-G-C-E♭-G-C - see measure 9) left hand patterns.

by **Jerald Simon**

MM00001016

Destiny

MM00001016

Destiny

Destiny

MM00001016

Resolution

This piano solo uses a *1-5-8-9-10* (eg. C-G-C-D-E - see measure 1) left hand pattern as well as a few others. See if you can figure out the other left hand patterns used in this piece!

Tenderly (♩ = c. 105)

by **Jerald Simon**

pedal ad-lib throughout

MM00001016

Resolution

Resolution

Resolution

My Mission: (*My Primary Music Motivation® Goal*): Create fun, original piano music that is cool, exciting, entertaining, and educational to help motivate and inspire piano students! (especially teenage boys)!

My Music Motivation® Goal (for music educators): One of my primary goals at Music Motivation® is to help prepare the next generation of composers, arrangers, musicians, music teachers, and musicologists to use their music and their love of music to make a difference in their own lives, their community, and the world.

Music Motivation® is dedicated to motivating music students of all ages with "Music that excites, entertains, and educates"™. The three main areas of focus for Music Motivation® are: Theory Therapy™, Innovative Improvisation™, and Creative Composition™.

MM00001016

Every week Jerald produces and releases a new "Cool Song" available for all piano students and piano teachers on his website (*musicmotivation.com*). Each new *"Cool Song"* is emailed to Music Motivation® mentees (piano teachers and piano students) according to their preferred subscription. See which subscription is the best fit for you and for your piano students (if you are a piano teacher) by visiting:

http://musicmotivation.com/annualsubscription

At Music Motivation®, I strive to produce the best quality products I can to help musicians of all ages better understand music theory (Theory Therapy™), improvisation (Innovative Improvisation™), and composition (Creative Composition™). I try to tailor my products around the needs of piano teachers and piano students of all ages - from beginning through advanced and would love to receive your feedback about what I can do to better help you teach and learn. Let me know if there is a type of piano music, music book, fun audio or video tutorial, or any other educational product you would like to see in the field of music (principally the piano), but have not yet found, that would help you teach and learn the paino better. Please contact me. I look forward to your comments and suggestions. Thank you.

Testimonials about Jerald
here are a few testimonials from musicians and piano teachers

"Jerald's hymn arrangements are as beautiful as they are musically interesting. I'm sure people are going to love hearing them in church meetings or wherever they are played."

- Jon Schmidt - Piano Guys

"Jerald is a wonderful human being who has inspired not only me to be a better pianist, but hundreds of other people. Keep up all the great work Jerald."

- Paul Cardall - Music Producer, Film Composer, Recording Artist

"What I love about arrangements of well-sung songs done by various artists is that one can hear the pianist's personality come through in a very real and intimate way. Jerald's passion for life and his beliefs comes through in his unique and distinctive arrangements of these well-known religious hymns."

- Kurt Bestor (Owner, Kurt Bestor Music)

"Jerald Simon's arrangement of A Poor Wayfaring Man of Grief is peaceful and soothing. It is not rushed, allowing lines to breathe and resolve. He continues to produce music that will bring spiritual comfort to those who are listening."

- Josh Wright (concert pianist and online piano teacher)

"Jerald Simon is a brilliant musician, teacher, and performer, with a fascinating story to tell. If you're interested in learning how to improvise or compose music, be sure to check out his books."

- Brandon Pearce - Owner, Music Teacher's Helper, LLC

"Jerald's motivational poetry, writing and music education books are a true expression of Jerald's winning personality and innovation. He is a Utah treasure."

- David Burger, Music critic, arts reporter, Salt Lake Tribune

"Not only do you get a song per week to learn, but all of the "fixings" (supplements) to go with it! Backing tracks, PDFs and also a step by step video going though each song. Wow! It's a great value for the price. I think students would enjoy playing these (cool) songs. Teachers and students shouldn't think twice about learning about (Jerald's) compositions and letting themselves be inspired by his musical style. Don't delay - jump in today!"

- Jeff Willie - Piano Teacher

"My favorite thing about the "Cool Songs" is the music theory that is introduced in the YouTube videos. So many times, students don't understand the why behind theory until they have been taking lessons for several years. The videos introduce theory concepts in a way that compliments the song, and then gives students a reason to actually use it!" Thanks again!

-Amanda W Smith (Piano Teacher - Founder of modernmusicteaching.com

Learn more about

JERALD SIMON

Visit **http://musicmotivation.com/jeraldsimon**

"My purpose and mission in life is to motivate myself and others through my music and writing, to help others find their purpose and mission in life, and to teach values that encourage everyone everywhere to do and be their best." - Jerald Simon

First and foremost, Jerald is a husband to his beautiful wife, Zanny, and a father to his wonderful children. Jerald Simon is the founder and president of Music Motivation® (**musicmotivation.com**). He is a composer, author, poet, and Music Mentor/piano teacher (primarily focusing his piano teaching on music theory, and encouraging students with improvisation, composition, and arranging). Jerald loves music, teaching, speaking, performing, playing sports, exercising, gardening (he's a wannabe gardner) reading, writing poetry and self help books, and spending time with his wife, Zanny, and their children.

Jerald created **musicmotivation.com** as a resource for piano teachers, piano students, and parents of piano students. He is the author/poet of "The As If Principle" (222 motivational poems), and "Perceptions, Parables, and Pointers." He is also the author of 20 music books from the Music Motivation® Series (over 200 plus original piano solos between the books) including the popular series: Cool Songs for Cool Kids (pre-primer, primer level, and volumes 1, 2, and 3) and Cool Songs that Rock (books 1 and 2) which all feature original piano music Jerald has composed primarily with teenage boys in mind. He has also recorded and produced several albums and singles of original music as well as hymn arrangements. In 2014, Jerald started a "Cool Songs" annual subscription on his website where he produces and releases one new "Cool Song" for the piano every week with minus tracks (accompaniment parts), the PDF download, MP3 downloads, and a YouTube video tutorial where he teaches the "Cool Song" and music theory the fun way. Watch his videos on his website at http://musicmotivation.com/annualsubscription, and check out his videos at http://youtube.com/jeraldsimon

Jerald also presents to various music schools, groups, and associations throughout the country doing various workshops, music camps, master classes, concerts and firesides to inspire and motivate teens, adults, music students and teachers. He enjoys teaching piano students about music theory, improvisation, and composition. He refers to himself as a Music Mentor and encourages music students to get motivated by music and to motivate others through music of their own.

SPECIALTIES:

Composer, Author, Poet, Music Mentor, Piano Teacher (focusing primarily on jazz, music theory, improvisation, composition, arranging, etc.), Motivational Speaker, and life coach. Please visit this link: **http://musicmotivation.com/speaker**, to book Jerald as a speaker/performer. You may also visit **http://musicmotivation.com/resources** to print off FREE piano resources for piano teachers and piano students.

www.ingramcontent.com/pod-product-compliance
Lightning Source LLC
LaVergne TN
LVHW061340060426
835511LV00014B/2039